BOOK OF
TWENTY ONE
RULES

planet π2

First published in Great Britain
in 2014 by PlanetK2

Copyright © PlanetK2 2014

A CIP Catalogue of this book is available from the British Library.

ISBN: 978-0-9927598-4-1

Cover design and typeset by
www.chandlerbookdesign.co.uk

Printed in Great Britain by
CPI Group (UK) Ltd, Croydon CR0 4YY

Welcome to the
book of rules

Inspired by the fabulous Velominati we've annointed ourselves as the
Performerati, keepers of the human performance rules.

These are the rules. You can choose to respect, uphold, share,
nurture and protect them. If you do, then you will be part of a small band
of people who choose to pursue excellence in performance.
The alternative is to pursue mediocrity. As ever, performance is a choice.

The Performance Geek is Keeper of the Rules and can
be contacted at performancegeek@planetK2.com

#1

It never gets easier, you just perform better

You have a duty to be dissatisfied with the status quo, however great that is. You must always look for areas of improvement unless you consider yourself to be the finished article in which case see Rule 20.

#2

Love the one you're with

Some choose to become experts at describing the conditions and how tough and unfair they are. It's an interesting expertise though not a particularly useful one. You learn to love or embrace the conditions you're in, whatever they are, because that's what it takes.

#3

There is a correct answer

There's no such thing as a stupid question (though some get pretty close) but there are some really stupid answers. Bloke down the pub conversations don't count as evidence however many quizzes you've won. 40 years of research is there for a reason. Everyone's got an opinion on human performance and motivation. A few of those people actually know what they're talking about.

#4

Be boring

Be great at the basics - raft building, walking over hot coals or breaking arrows has nothing to do with performance. It may be entertaining but if it's entertainment you're after, go to the cinema. Get great at the basics of doing your job, making sure your technical and tactical skills are superb and relevant. Then get great at the other basics - your mentality, your energy levels, your support team and your environment.

#5

Talent is overrated, hard work isn't

Everyone has talent, but what you do with it and how you grow it is what makes a difference. Hard work beats talent when talent doesn't work hard. Relying on your strengths is lazy. Knowing them, valuing them and building them is what matters.

#6

You're on a talent development programme

Whether you like it or not. If you haven't been invited onto the formal talent development programme because you're too small, too big, your face doesn't fit, you don't know the right people or you're lazy then put your own programme together. If you're not invited because you have nothing to offer then see Rule 20.

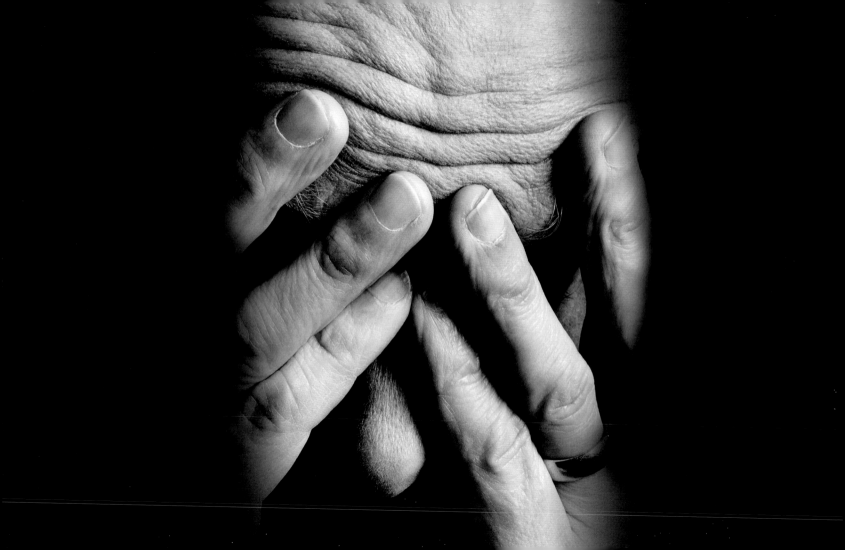

#7

Don't motivate people

It's a waste of time and space. Instead help them remember why they're doing it, why they should be confident and to focus on the things they can control.

#8

It may not be your fault, though you are responsible

For your attitude, motivation, development, diet, exercise, actions, behaviours and performance. If someone else is responsible for these things on your behalf, do something about it or fire yourself.

#9

If you have the word leader in your title then you are doubly responsible

Leadership is a behaviour not a title. You lead through
your attitude, your choices, your responses and your body
language. Your own feelings are secondary to those you
lead. If that seems hard then see Rules 20 and 21.

If you're going to have party food at your meetings, then invite Coco the clown

Chocolate biscuits, jelly babies, cake - why not give them a party bag too? Have you seen kids at a birthday party? Is that how you want to fuel something that's costing your business a fortune? Really?

#11

HR's job is to lead on helping people perform better, not be happier

If you want to just make people happier and make sure they're having fun then fill your boots and enjoy being overtaken by other organisations that are full of people who have a different sort of happiness - the happiness that comes from getting better, not from bringing your dog to work day or going to the company BBQ.

#12

Being obsessed with measuring everything is totally bonkers

Obsessing on stuff is ok and not as bad as it's cracked up to be, but obsessing on the wrong stuff is just stupid.

#13

Teams in search of a purpose are strictly forbidden

If you're on a team and you're not sure why the team exists, then sort it out now or disband. Teams in search of a purpose are a waste of space, oxygen and shareholder funds.

#14

Relentless positivity is silly and annoying

It may work for you and that's fine. Negative thinking may work for others and that's fine too. The only thing that matters is whether it helps performance. Do you really want the person who maintains the next aircraft you fly on to be a relentlessly positive thinker? "Yeah, sure it'll be fine…."

#15

Everyone has a Performance Improvement Plan

If you do a job then getting better at it is a non-negotiable part of your role. Performance improvement is not remedial; it's a way of life. If you don't have a performance improvement plan then see Rule 20. Oh and waiting for HR, L&D or anyone else to do it for you is ridiculous - you're not a helpless puppy.

#16

Sticks are for dogs to chase

Goals are only to be used to help motivation and performance.
Not to hit people with.

#17

Performance is performance.
Results are not.

Performance is about doing the things you need to do in order to get the things you want. If you want results, then you need to know how to perform. Wanting results by talking about results is like thinking that the best way to get hold of cake is to talk about cake. You're probably better off going down the shops.

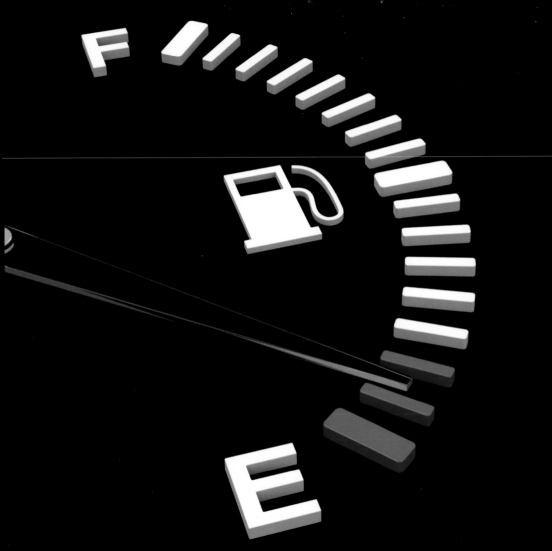

#18

Indicators are not targets

The clue is in the name. Indicators indicate things - they point out where you are or where you're heading. The fuel gauge in your car is an indicator (and clearly so are the indicators). The place you're travelling to is the target. If you want key result targets then you are to call them KRTs. Otherwise KPIs are KPIs.

#19

Be a boy scout.

Be prepared. Great performance means you need to be constantly ready to perform in all conditions. Know what you need to be ready for, what you need to do to be ready and then practice it. Starting now.

#20

Your job is to uphold the rules or fire yourself

If you can't or won't then see Rule 21.

#21

HTFU

www.planetK2.com

www.theperformanceroom.co.uk

twitter PlanetK2

linkedin PlanetK2

facebook PlanetK2

...because talent is not enough